THIS BOOK IS THE PROPERTY OF
PATTISHALL C E PRIMARY SCHOOL
2022

GREENPEACE

By Kirsty Holmes

BookLife PUBLISHING

©2018
BookLife Publishing
King's Lynn
Norfolk PE30 4LS

All rights reserved.
Printed in Malaysia.

A catalogue record for this book is available from the British Library.

ISBN: 978-1-78637-316-8

Written by:
Kirsty Holmes

Edited by:
Madeline Tyler

Designed by:
Dan Scase

All facts, statistics, web addresses and URLs in this book were verified as valid and accurate at time of writing. No responsibility for any changes to external websites or references can be accepted by either the author or publisher.

Page 4
CHARITY & GIVING

Page 6
GREENPEACE

Page 10
THE NATURAL WORLD

Page 13
PEACE & WAR

Page 14
DEFEND THE NATURAL WORLD: TIME

Page 16
DEFEND THE NATURAL WORLD: MONEY

Page 18
DEFEND THE NATURAL WORLD: ACTIVISM

Page 20
SUCCESS STORY: MICROBEADS

Page 22
SUCCESS STORY: SANCTUARY IN ANTARCTICA

Page 24
THE ART OF PROTEST

Page 26
GET INVOLVED

Page 30
FIND OUT MORE

Page 31
GLOSSARY

Page 32
INDEX

Words that look like **THIS** are explained in the glossary on page 31.

CHARITY & GIVING

Some people give money to charity.

WHAT IS 'CHARITY'?

Every person and animal on planet Earth is part of a **GLOBAL COMMUNITY**. We all need similar things to survive and grow. Every person needs food to eat, fresh water to drink and somewhere safe to live.

But, even though we all need the same things, we don't all have the same things. Some people and animals have access to more **RESOURCES** or are better protected from danger than others.

For example, in some countries there may not be enough food for people to eat, or there may be wars or natural disasters which have taken away people's homes. People are also in danger all over the world from illness, injury and disease.

Some people give their time to help others.

Many people see these problems and feel a strong need to make it better. They help by giving time, money or other resources, such as food, to those in need. This type of giving is called charity.

Some people help animals in danger, like orangutans.

WHAT IS A CHARITY?

When a group of people get together and form an organisation to help people, animals or other good causes, we call that organisation a charity. Charities can be huge, **INTERNATIONAL** organisations with thousands of people working for them, or they can be small groups working for a local good cause. People donate their time and money to charities, and in turn, the charities organise these resources to help people in the best way possible.

Some charities are like big companies, organising thousands of people and millions of pounds.

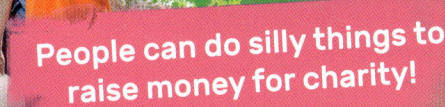

People can do silly things to raise money for charity!

Small local charities, like hospices or animal sanctuaries, rely on people's donations.

KEY WORDS ABOUT CHARITIES

- **Donation** — a gift of time, money or goods to a charity
- **Donor** — a person or company who makes a donation
- **Volunteer** — a person who works for a charity but isn't paid
- **Fundraising** — collecting money for a charity
- **Awareness** — making sure people know about a charity or issue
- **Campaign** — work in an organised way towards a goal
- **Activist** — person who campaigns and raises awareness on a topic

GREENPEACE

THE GREENPEACE CORE VALUES

For a Green and Peaceful Planet

Greenpeace is an independent campaigning organisation, which uses non-violent, creative confrontation to expose global environmental problems, and to force the solutions which are essential to a green and peaceful future.

Greenpeace's goal is to ensure the ability of the Earth to nurture life in all its diversity.

Therefore Greenpeace seeks to:

- Protect **BIODIVERSITY** in all its forms
- Prevent pollution and abuse of the Earth's ocean, land, air and fresh water
- End all nuclear threats
- Promote peace, global disarmament and non-violence

Greenpeace seeks solutions for, and promotes open, informed debate about society's environmental choices. They don't work to manage environmental problems, they work to eliminate them.

"It's not enough for us to point the finger; we develop, research and promote concrete steps towards a green and peaceful future for all of us."

Core values, or a mission statement, tell you what a charity stands for, who they want to help, and why.

Find out more about Greenpeace's mission at: https://www.greenpeace.org/archive-international/en/about/our-core-values/#a0

DEFENDING THE NATURAL WORLD

Greenpeace's creative protests are very eye-catching and help start conversations.

Greenpeace is known for its creative protests and has been called 'the most visible environmental organisation in the world'.

HOW GREENPEACE BEGAN

Greenpeace is a charity and organisation working to defend the natural world and promote peace. They work to fight against the destruction of the natural environment, stop climate change, and promote a peaceful world without **NUCLEAR WEAPONS**.

In the 1960s, US nuclear weapon tests were growing in frequency and power. Nuclear weapon tests are very dangerous for the environment and also for people living nearby, and many people protested against them. Jim Bohlen, and Irving and Dorothy Stowe, had the idea to sail a boat to the site of the tests and try to stop them through the idea of 'passive resistance' – that just by witnessing and talking about the tests, they could draw attention and get them stopped. They organised a concert to raise the money, bought a boat, and named it Greenpeace. They sailed to the site of the tests, but were turned back. However, when they got home, they found that their voyage had drawn a lot of attention, and people agreed with them. Eventually, after many such voyages, **PUBLIC OPINION** stopped the tests, and Greenpeace the movement was born.

"It is amazing what a few people sitting around their kitchen table can achieve." – Dorothy Stowe, Greenpeace Founder

This map shows (in green) countries where Greenpeace have offices.

Three of the Founding Members of Greenpeace in 1971 – the Don't Make a Wave Committee.

WHAT DOES GREENPEACE DO?

Greenpeace work to defend the natural world and promote peace. They do this by investigating environmental problems, speaking out globally about them, and protesting directly to protect the natural environment. They are focused on the following main areas:

STOP CLIMATE CHANGE

Greenpeace work to stop climate change, promoting environmentally friendly alternatives and new technologies and solutions.

DEFEND THE OCEANS

Greenpeace campaign to stop overfishing, pollution and climate change, and protect the seas.

PROTECT THE FORESTS

Greenpeace work to stop **DEFORESTATION** and protect forests.

WORK FOR PEACE

Greenpeace believe that all countries with nuclear weapons should give them up, and focus on building a peaceful future.

DETOX

Greenpeace work to get rid of **TOXIC** chemicals from the natural world.

SAVE THE ARCTIC

Greenpeace work to stop climate change and prevent oil companies drilling in the Arctic for oil.

The Famous Greenpeace Flagship, the Rainbow Warrior

Since its beginning, Greenpeace has grown into an international organisation, and employs over 2,400 people across the world, as well as an amazing 15,000 volunteers and activists. Greenpeace are an instantly recognisable organisation, with their famous flagship the Rainbow Warrior, and their creative, visual and active approach to protesting and defending the environment.

This is a Greenpeace protest in support of solar power and renewables in Ljubljana, Slovenia.

GREENPEACE FACT FILE

- **Charity Name:** Greenpeace
- **Also Known As:** Greenpeace International
- **Started:** 1971 in Vancouver, Canada
- **Staff:** 2,400
- **Countries Helped:** Worldwide
- **Yearly Budget:** Over €236.9 Million Euros
- **Main Areas:** Environmental issues and nuclear disarmament
- **Fundraising:** Donations only - no businesses or government funding

Find out more at
www.greenpeace.org

THE NATURAL WORLD

There are many threats facing our natural world. Climate change is altering habitats and **MIGRATION** patterns for lots of animals, causing many to become **ENDANGERED**. Forests are being destroyed to make way for **AGRICULTURE**, and we are pouring plastic waste and toxic chemicals into the oceans. If we do not take urgent action to stop these things happening, our natural environment and the resources we need to survive could be lost forever.

NATURAL DISASTERS

There are many things contributing to climate change, but scientists agree that many of them are caused by humans and their activities. The burning of fossil fuels – coal, oil and gas – is causing carbon dioxide and greenhouse gases to build up in the atmosphere. This is made worse as we destroy the rainforests, which remove carbon dioxide from the atmosphere. These gases trap heat on the planet, causing the Earth's temperature to rise. No one knows how much warming of the planet is 'safe', but we do know that climate change is already harming people and the environment all over the world.

Climate change causes extreme weather to occur, like Hurricane Harvey, which hit the East Coast of the USA in 2017 and caused huge destruction across a large area.

Climate change is causing the ice at the Earth's poles to melt. This is a disaster for the natural wildlife in the area.

DEFORESTATION

Forests are the most diverse ECOSYSTEMS on Earth and are home to millions of species of plants and animals. The Amazon Rainforest alone is home to almost half of all known species on the planet. However, humans have destroyed over 80 percent of the world's forests.

Many forests are protected areas, but that doesn't stop illegal LOGGING from taking place. Deforestation – the destruction of a natural forest – happens to clear land for farming or to use the wood for building or trade.

This area of rainforest in Guyana, South America, has been cleared to make way for a gold mine. Mining is very destructive to the environment.

SAVE OUR SEAS

The oceans and seas that make up over 70% of the Earth's surface are under threat from climate change, overfishing, and pollution. One of the biggest problems facing the oceans at the moment is from plastic pollution. An estimated 12.7 million tonnes of plastic – from plastic bottles and bags to microbeads – goes into the ocean each year. That's the equivalent of one truck-load of rubbish every minute. Plastic bags have been found in the stomachs of turtles and whales, and every species, from tiny zooplankton to huge whales, are affected.

Sea turtles like to eat jellyfish, and often mistake floating plastic bags for their favourite food.

Find out more about microbeads on page 20.

Can you tell the difference?

Bees pollinate over a third of all the plant food that humans eat. **PESTICIDES** kill bees and harm their populations.

TOXIC CHEMICALS

Toxic chemicals used in **MANUFACTURING** and as pesticides have a terrible effect on the environment. Factories using poisonous chemicals in their work can pollute surrounding water supplies, leak into the soil, and **CONTAMINATE** drinking water for people living near these factories. Chemicals used as pesticides can contaminate soil and crops, and endanger wildlife, such as the bees we depend on to **POLLINATE** the plants we eat.

Greenteam kids protest to protect the bees.

SAVE THE ARCTIC

The ecosystem in the arctic is a fragile and endangered place. Melting polar ice is already under threat from climate change, caused by the burning of fossil fuels like oil. As Arctic ice melts, oil companies have started moving in to drill for more oil, making the problem even worse. As there is only a brief period of the year when the Arctic can be reached, if there was an oil spill, it would be almost impossible to deal with and would destroy huge parts of this beautiful place.

An Abandoned Drilling Tower in the Arctic

PEACE & WAR

WHAT ARE NUCLEAR WEAPONS?

Nuclear weapons are the most powerful bombs that humans have ever invented. They produce massive, destructive explosions, and spread **RADIOACTIVITY** over a wide area. Only two nuclear weapons have ever been used in war – the ones dropped on the cities of Hiroshima and Nagasaki in Japan, at the end of World War II. Since then, much larger and more powerful bombs have been designed, although never used in war.

The Nuclear Explosions over Hiroshima and Nagasaki in 1945

WHY ARE NUCLEAR WEAPONS BAD?

Even though only two nuclear weapons have been used in war, many more have been tested since then. The destruction to the environment and the oceans after a nuclear test is huge, and the radioactivity can linger for many years. As long as countries have nuclear weapons, there is always the risk that they can get into the wrong hands, or could be used in a nuclear war. Greenpeace believe that the only way to be sure this won't happen is for all countries to agree to give up their nuclear weapons.

This corn, grown from seeds exposed to atomic radiation, shows the effects. Can you see the strange-shaped kernels?

A Nuclear Weapons Test in 1951

DEFEND THE NATURAL WORLD

TIME

Greenpeace strongly believe that people can learn to live peacefully in the natural world. They believe in protecting and defending the natural world so we can share it with animals – and each other – long into the future. They work all over the world to educate people, and cause real change to happen.

This crew member is aboard the Rainbow Warrior ship.

PEOPLE

One of the most important resources a charity can have is people giving their time. From volunteers working for free, to paid, full-time employees, the time people give to protect the planet, raise awareness and fight for peace is very important to any charity.

These Greenpeace volunteers are working to clean up an oil spill in Usinsk, Russia.

VOLUNTEERS

Volunteers give their time to a charity for free. Locally, this could be campaigning, raising awareness or fundraising. Greenpeace volunteers work in central and local offices, work to **LOBBY** governments, help to raise funds in the streets, and even participate in non-violent direct action (NVDA) – protesting directly at sites or taking part in one of their eye-catching campaigns.

Greenpeace sends out approximately 15,000 international volunteers every year.

WORKING FOR GREENPEACE

Greenpeace employ many types of paid staff. From working in local and national offices, working aboard a ship, **POLITICAL ADVISORS**, to staff working in warehouses and on campaigns, there are many ways to make protecting the planet a full-time job.

There are many ways people can work for a charity and have a career that will help others.

DEFEND THE NATURAL WORLD

FINANCIAL INDEPENDENCE

MONEY

Charities need money to be able to do their work. But where do they get it from?

It's very important to Greenpeace that they stay independent of any company, government or **POLITICAL PARTY**. This is because Greenpeace will campaign on very specific issues – sometimes working to stop a particular company from cutting down forests or polluting the environment, or asking a government to invest in renewables. If Greenpeace took money from these organisations, they could feel pressured to change the way they campaign or work, and they don't want to do that. So instead, they get all their money from donations.

Find out more about donating to Greenpeace at https://greenpeace.org.uk/ and click the 'donate' button.

Fundraising is often done by volunteers.

DONATIONS

People can donate money to Greenpeace just once, or they can send a regular payment from their bank account. People could also choose to leave money in their **WILL** after they die. Greenpeace check all their donations and cheques to make sure they are not coming from companies, and if they are, they actually send them back! This is to make sure there is absolutely no **CORRUPTION** and they are free to defend the natural world wherever they need to.

FUNDRAISING

Greenpeace rely on people raising money to support the charity's work. People can raise money in lots of ways – from getting sponsored to run a marathon to hosting a cake sale. Raising money is important and fun and it means Greenpeace can continue campaigning for a green and peaceful planet.

LEGACIES

When someone dies, they usually have a will, which is a document they write before they die, deciding what will happen to their possessions after they have gone. Many people leave their money to family members or friends, but some people leave some money to charity too. This is called a legacy donation, and can be a way that someone can make sure their beliefs are supported even after they have gone. Legacy donations now pay for 1 in 6 of Greenpeace's campaigns.

DEFENDING THE NATURAL WORLD

ACTIVISM

As well as providing medical care, Greenpeace has a policy of non-violence and bearing witness. This means that, as well as campaigning, writing letters and filling **PETITIONS**, Greenpeace volunteers and staff also travel directly to places where they are needed, sometimes directly standing in the way of environmental damage. Greenpeace activists have a name for this: non-violent direct action (NVDA). Greenpeace activists who do this are carefully trained and know the risks of this type of action. They are taught to stay calm, and understand that they are likely to be arrested.

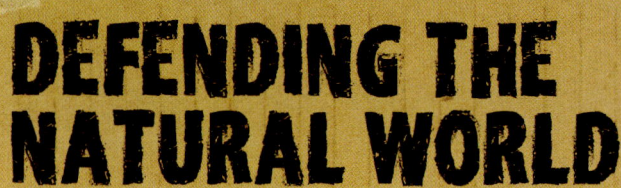

This Greenpeace activist has her arm locked inside an `arm bar' which is locked to an excavator. She is standing in the way of a company who are trying to cut down part of a rainforest.

SOCIAL MEDIA

Social media is a very powerful tool in raising awareness. Greenpeace uses social media to raise awareness, share stories and successes, and let people know about their work and the problems facing people and the environment around the world. Some of what they share on social media might be upsetting for you – think about asking an adult, like a parent or teacher, with an account on one of these sites to show you Greenpeace's work, and talk with you about what you see there.

@Greenpeaceuk

@greenpeaceuk

@greenpeaceuk

Greenpeace UK

18

"What made me feel so passionate about the work of Greenpeace was talking with scientists and realising, while standing on a melting ice cap, how close we really are to disaster... We cannot take anything for granted in such a dangerous era. We have to make our mark. We have to speak. We have to act. And we have to act together."
EMMA THOMPSON, ACTRESS AND ACTIVIST

The ecosystem of the Arctic is very important to the climate, and must be protected.

Emma Thompson

Actress Emma Thompson is a vocal supporter of Greenpeace, amongst other activist groups and charities. She gave a speech and helped in a very interesting protest in which a giant polar bear puppet, called Aurora, was left outside the headquarters of an oil company called Shell. Aurora was put in place in London to protest against Shell's activities drilling for oil in the Arctic. Aurora was the size of a double decker bus! After a month, Shell announced that they were going to stop drilling for oil in the Arctic, and so Aurora was taken away in a celebratory parade and taken to Paris, where important climate talks were taking place. Creative protests like these help draw people's attention to particular causes, and public pressure and opinion can be very powerful in getting companies to change their minds about the way they do things.

Find out more about Emma Thompson's work with Greenpeace at www.greenpeace.org.uk and search for Emma Thompson.

SUCCESS STORY: MICROBEADS

Plastic microbeads are found in cosmetics.

WHAT ARE MICROBEADS?

Microbeads are tiny little pieces of plastic. For years, they have been included in toothpastes, face and body scrubs, and other cosmetics as an exfoliator – something that helps scrub away dead skin cells. They were also used in some medical and health science research.

WHAT'S THE PROBLEM?

Microbeads are washed down the sink with your face scrub or toothpaste. This means they quickly enter the water system. Because they are so tiny – less than one millimetre (mm) in size – it's very hard to filter them out in water treatment plants, so they end up in natural waterways, rivers, and eventually the sea. They then enter the food chain because **MARINE** creatures think they are food – microbeads look similar to tiny plankton and algae that small fish and turtles like to eat. If animals accidentally eat the plastic, it can't be digested, and builds up inside the animals' stomachs. If their stomachs are full of plastic, they can't digest food properly. This can lead to poisoning, or death. Microbeads can even enter the human food chain if we eat the fish and shellfish which have plastic in them.

This larvae of a perch (a type of fish), seen here under a microscope, already has tiny plastic particles in it's stomach and intestines. Can you spot them?

Adult Perch

BAN THE BEAD

Worldwide, there have been a number of different campaigns protesting against the use of these tiny plastics in cosmetics.

In the UK, Greenpeace worked with other campaign groups and charities to persuade the UK government to ban the use and sale of microbeads, and to ban anyone from making any more of them. Greenpeace used a petition to show the UK government that the people supported their campaign – 350,000 people signed it! This was the largest environmental petition that the government had ever received.

Cosmetics contribute to the 12 million tonnes of plastic that ends up in the sea every year.

It took two years of protests, petitions and campaigns, but in January 2018 the UK government banned the use of microbeads in 'rinse-off' cosmetics – like toothpaste, shower gel or face scrubs.

STILL MORE TO DO

After the ban, companies can still put plastic into products that are 'leave-on' such as sun protection cream or makeup, or some cleaning products. Greenpeace know that until no more plastic is going into the sea, the fight for the oceans goes on.

Greenpeace youth activists in Hamburg, Germany, made a huge wooden bottle to protest against the microplastics in cosmetics.

SUCCESS STORY: SANCTUARY IN ANTARCTICA

This map shows the seas of Antarctica. Can you find the Ross Sea?

THE ROSS SEA

The Ross Sea is a deep bay in the Antarctic Ocean, and includes a large area of ice known as the Ross Ice Shelf. The Ross Sea lies around 320 kilometres (km) from the South Pole. In total, the Ross Sea is over 1.5 million square km of beautiful, biodiverse ocean which is almost totally unexplored and unspoiled. That's an area three times the size of Texas – or twice the size of Spain!

The Ross Sea is home to more than:
- 10 Mammal Species
- 6 Bird Species
- 95 Fish Species
- 1,000 **INVERTEBRATE** Species

The Ross Sea is sometimes called "The Last Ocean" because it is almost completely untouched and unaffected by human activity. Because the water is so deep and moves very slowly, it stays relatively warm and this makes a very good habitat for many species of marine life.

The water here is special because it is very rich in **NUTRIENTS**. This means lots of plankton and krill can grow here. The plankton and krill provide food for other animals such as whales, seals and birds. Fish which eat the krill in turn become food for the Adélie and emperor penguins who breed and live in this area. In 2007, a 10-metre long colossal squid was found in these waters too.

Weddell Seals

Snow Petrel

Minke Whale

Orca

Antarctic Krill

Adélie Penguins

MARINE PROTECTED AREA

For many years, discussions have been taking place at the Commission for the Conservation of Antarctic Marine Living Resources (CCAMLR), an organisation which forms part of an agreement between many countries about the Antarctic and its resources. These discussions focused on how and when to make the Ross Sea into a Marine Protected Area (MPA). An MPA is an area of sea which is protected by laws from human activity. After many years of campaigning, including activity from Greenpeace in calling on governments to vote for the MPA to happen, in October 2016 the CCAMLR declared the Ross Sea as an MPA.

This satellite image shows the 'bloom' of plankton (in green) in the Ross Sea. Plankton is an essential part of the food chain, and will be protected in the MPA.

SANCTUARY IN ANTARCTICA

The Ross Sea Marine Protected Area is now the biggest MPA in the world! Fishing will no longer be allowed in most of this this area, which will help to protect the Antarctic toothfish – a predator fish which is popular in Chile. The small amount of fishing that is allowed will be carefully monitored. This is known as a 'no-take zone' meaning humans can no longer take from this area. Important habitats for penguins, seals and birds are also protected.

It was a huge victory for Greenpeace to be able to play such a big part in achieving this and safeguarding the MPA in the Ross Sea. Because the agreement only lasts 35 years, they know they will need to monitor this and make sure that, when 35 years is up, it's an easy decision to protect this special part of the world forever.

These activists marched dressed as penguins to support the MPA in the Ross Sea.

THE ART OF PROTEST

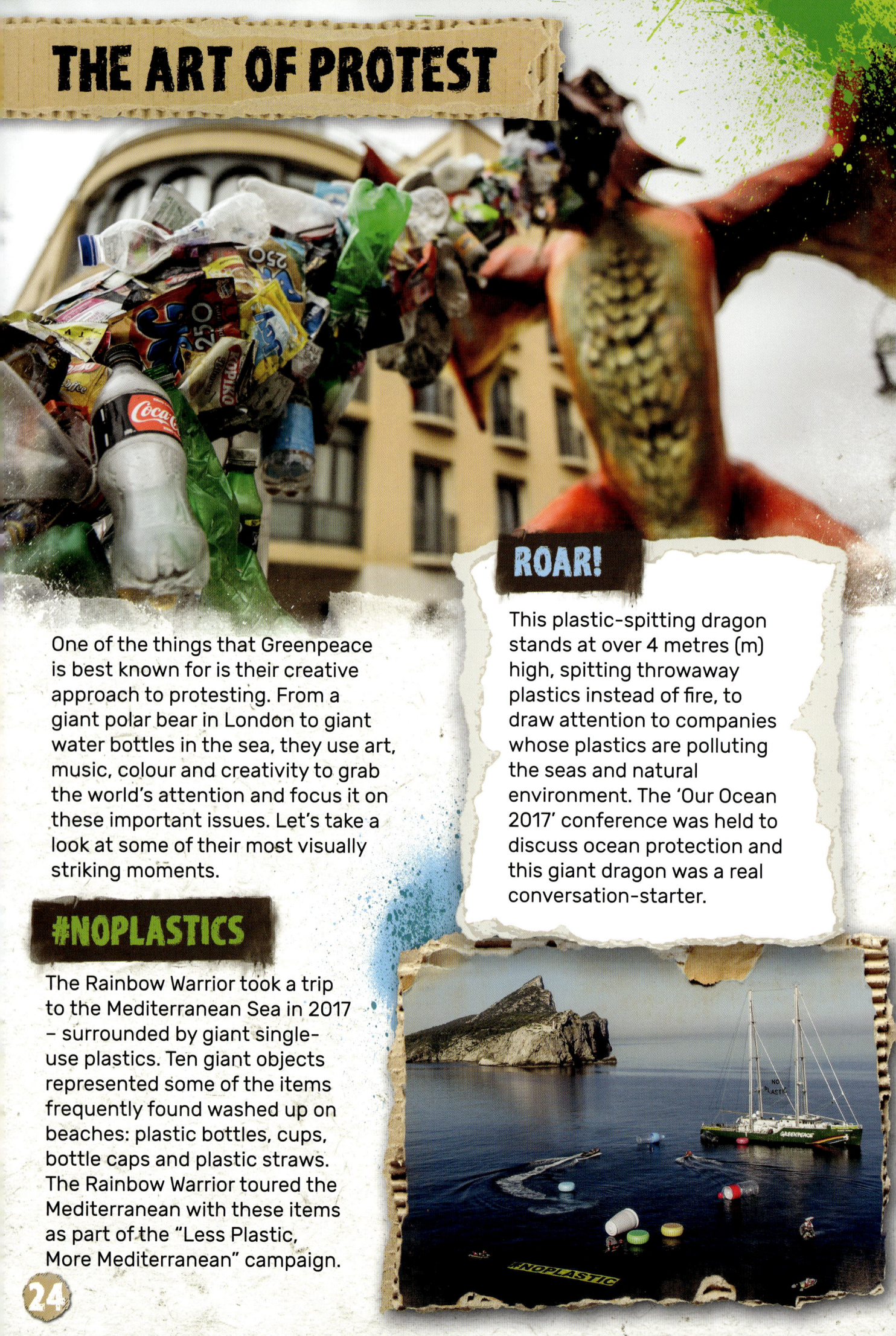

One of the things that Greenpeace is best known for is their creative approach to protesting. From a giant polar bear in London to giant water bottles in the sea, they use art, music, colour and creativity to grab the world's attention and focus it on these important issues. Let's take a look at some of their most visually striking moments.

ROAR!

This plastic-spitting dragon stands at over 4 metres (m) high, spitting throwaway plastics instead of fire, to draw attention to companies whose plastics are polluting the seas and natural environment. The 'Our Ocean 2017' conference was held to discuss ocean protection and this giant dragon was a real conversation-starter.

#NOPLASTICS

The Rainbow Warrior took a trip to the Mediterranean Sea in 2017 – surrounded by giant single-use plastics. Ten giant objects represented some of the items frequently found washed up on beaches: plastic bottles, cups, bottle caps and plastic straws. The Rainbow Warrior toured the Mediterranean with these items as part of the "Less Plastic, More Mediterranean" campaign.

London

Sydney

MARCH OF THE PENGUINS

In January 2018, something odd was happening. From Sydney, Australia to London, UK, penguins started travelling on trains, arriving at airports and posing at landmarks – including the Sydney Opera House, Berlin's Brandenburg Gate, and Platform 9 ¾ at King's Cross! These travelling penguins caused a stir, but they were on the march to ensure the MPA in the Ross Sea was finally approved after years of campaigning.

WHALE ART IN THE PHILIPPINES

This giant sculpture of a whale, choked by plastic pollution, was installed near Manila. Greenpeace used this sculpture to draw attention to the problem of plastics entering the food chain.

This aerial view of the No Plastic human banner action in Beirut, Lebanon, protests against plastic pollution. This beach in Raouche is polluted with lots of plastics.

Human Banner Action in Dakar, where Greenpeace and 400 local school children formed a human fish-shaped banner.

Activists use yellow parasols to create the word 'No!' in Venice, Italy. This protest was against plans to build a nuclear power plant.

Sometimes, the simplest things can be the most effective. Using human bodies to make a banner, then photographing it from the skies, creates a striking image.

GET INVOLVED

Maybe what you've found out about Greenpeace and the causes they support has inspired you to take action. Let's look at how you can make a difference and support them.

DO!

Could you or your school organise a fundraising event? How can you help support Greenpeace's work? Here are some ideas.

CLEAN UP YOUR ACT

Maybe your school could visit a beach or forest and remove all the plastic waste. Once the adults have cleaned it all, your class could build a sculpture and take photos to raise awareness – like the whale on page 25.

SELL, SELL, SELL!

Hold a cake sale and harness your flour power! Decorate biscuits and cakes in rainbows, peace doves or animal shapes, and ask if you can hold a sale at school.

DRESS FOR SUCCESS

Ask your teachers if you can hold a fancy-dress day to raise money for Greenpeace. How about a theme:

Safety first! Make sure that all the plastic goes into the recycling afterwards. And always take care on the beach – wear gloves, goggles and protective clothes for picking up litter and stay with your teachers.

Commotion in the Ocean!

Riot in the Rainforest!

Planet Defenders!

Stay safe – make sure an adult helps you organise your event.

DISCUSS!

Become a youth activist, and raise awareness in your own communities. Here are some ways to get people talking.

WRITE A LETTER

Write to your local paper, your local council or even your local **MEMBER OF PARLIAMENT (MP)**. Tell them about environmental issues in your area - litter, pollution, or even trees. You might not think one letter could make a difference, but it can. Tell your friends - maybe you could all write a letter?

BE IN THE BANNER

Could your class make a human banner about an environmental issue you feel passionate about? You can use the picture to start a conversation and raise awareness of issues – maybe there is a local issue near you? Your local paper might even print it!

You can tell a reporter about the issue you care about.

SOCIAL MEDIA

If the adults in your family have social media accounts, ask them to follow or subscribe to Greenpeace and to share and like the posts they see. Every shared post helps to raise awareness and helps Greenpeace to bear witness to what they see.

Find out more at: https://www.greenpeace.org.uk/what-you-can-do/fundraise/

Always use social media with an adult.

DONATE!

PENNIES FOR PLASTIC

Ask your teacher if you can put a plastic bottle in your classroom. Get people to put their loose change in it – when it's full, you can donate the money to help Greenpeace fight plastics. Don't forget to recycle the bottle afterwards!

Money, time or goods – everyone can contribute something.

A bigger bottle will hold even more pennies! Ask a teacher to help you count them up and send them to Greenpeace. Even small amounts can make a big difference in fighting plastic pollution.

GIVE A BIRTHDAY GIFT

You could ask your family and friends to give a donation to Greenpeace instead of getting you a present. This can be a small amount but you will make a huge difference. Or how about donating to a charity as a gift for someone else?

Donating to charity instead of getting a gift is a very kind thing to do, and you will feel rewarded to know that you are giving the gift of a beautiful planet!

Colour runs are a fun way to raise money!

SPONSOR ME!

Hold an event, take on a challenge, or do something amazing, and get people to sponsor you. Run, walk, climb, bounce, skip... it's up to you!

Find out how to invite a Greenspeaker to talk to your school at: https://www.greenpeace.org.uk/what-you-can-do/greenspeakers/

FALL ASLEEP IN CLASS

Ask your headteacher to hold a school sleepover and charge everyone for a spot! Watch movies and tell stories about the environment, and serve hot chocolate – no plastic cups, of course!

FIND OUT MORE

GREENPEACE:
https://www.greenpeace.org.uk/

MAKE A DONATION:
https://secure.greenpeace.org.uk/page/contribute

FUNDRAISING IDEAS:
https://greenpeace.org.uk/what-you-can-do/fundraise/

YOUR LOCAL GROUP:
https://greenpeace.org.uk/what-you-can-do/groups/

Remember, not everything on the Greenpeace website is OK for children to see – some of their work is very grown-up and might be upsetting to look at. Make sure you have an adult check it out first, or sit with you while you look.

Write to your local MP to tell them about climate change and show you care: https://www.writetothem.com/

GLOSSARY

ADMINISTRATORS	BEING IN CHARGE OF OR ORGANISING SOMETHING
AGRICULTURE	THE PRACTICE OF FARMING
BIODIVERSITY	WHEN AN AREA HAS A LOT OF DIFFERENT TYPES OF ANIMALS OR PLANTS
CONTAMINATE	TO MAKE SOMETHING UNCLEAN BY ADDING A POISONOUS OR POLLUTING SUBSTANCE TO IT
CORRUPTION	WHEN SOMEONE IN A POSITION OF POWER IS NEGATIVELY INFLUENCED, OFTEN BY MONEY
DEFORESTATION	THE CLEARING OF FOREST TO MAKE LAND AVAILABLE FOR USE
ECOSYSTEMS	A COMMUNITY OF LIVING THINGS, TOGETHER WITH THEIR ENVIRONMENT
ENDANGERED	WHEN A SPECIES IS AT RISK OF BECOMING EXTINCT
GLOBAL COMMUNITY	THE PEOPLE AND NATIONS OF THE WORLD
INTERNATIONAL	RELATING TO DIFFERENT COUNTRIES
INVERTEBRATE	AN ANIMAL THAT DOESN'T HAVE A BACKBONE
LOBBY	TO TRY AND GET SOMEONE IN A GOVERNMENT TO VOTE IN A CERTAIN WAY
LOGGING	THE CUTTING DOWN OF TREES IN ORDER TO USE THE WOOD
MANUFACTURING	MAKING LARGE QUANTITIES OF SOMETHING
MARINE	RELATING TO THE SEA
MEMBER OF PARLIAMENT (MP)	AN ELECTED REPRESENTATIVE IN THE HOUSE OF COMMONS
MIGRATION	THE SEASONAL MOVEMENT OF ANIMALS FROM ONE AREA TO ANOTHER
NUCLEAR WEAPONS	VERY DESTRUCTIVE WEAPONS THAT USE NUCLEAR ENERGY
NUTRIENTS	NATURAL SUBSTANCES THAT PLANTS AND ANIMALS NEED TO GROW AND STAY HEALTHY
PESTICIDES	CHEMICALS USED TO KILL ANIMALS AND INSECTS THAT DAMAGE CROPS
PETITIONS	A LIST OF SIGNATURES SHOWING PEOPLE WHO AGREE WITH A TOPIC OR PROTEST
POLITICAL ADVISORS	PEOPLE WHOSE JOB IT IS TO PROVIDE ADVICE ON GOVERNMENTS AND POLITICS
POLITICAL PARTY	AN ORGANISED GROUP OF PEOPLE WHO HAVE SIMILAR IDEAS ABOUT GOVERNMENT
POLLINATE	MOVE POLLEN FROM ONE FLOWER TO ANOTHER
PUBLIC OPINION	THE OPINION OF THE PEOPLE OF AN AREA OR COUNTRY ON A PARTICULAR TOPIC
RADIOACTIVITY	WHEN SOMETHING GIVES OFF HARMFUL PARTICLES OF RADIATION
RESOURCES	SUPPLIES OF MONEY, MATERIALS OR PEOPLE
TOXIC	POISONOUS, CORROSIVE OR OTHERWISE HARMFUL
WILL	A DOCUMENT DECIDING WHAT HAPPENS TO SOMEONE'S POSSESSIONS AFTER THEY DIE

INDEX

A
AMAZON RAINFOREST 11
ANTARCTICA 22-23
ARCTIC, THE 8, 12, 19
ARM BARS 18
AURORA 19

B
BIODIVERSITY 6, 11, 22
BOHLEN, JIM 7

C
CLIMATE CHANGE 7-8, 10-12, 19, 30

D
DEFORESTATION 8, 10-11, 16, 18
DONATIONS 5, 16-17, 28, 30

F
FISHING 8, 11, 23
FORESTS 8, 10-11, 16, 18, 26
FUNDRAISING 5, 9, 15, 17, 26-27, 30

G
GLOBAL WARMING 10
GOVERNMENTS 9, 15-16, 21, 23

L
LEGACIES 17

M
MARINE PROTECTED AREAS (MPAS) 23, 25

N
NON-VIOLENT DIRECT ACTION (NVDA) 15, 18
NUCLEAR WEAPONS 6-9, 13

O
OIL 8, 10, 12, 14, 19
ORGANISATIONS 5-7, 9, 16, 23

P
PEACE 6-8, 13-14, 17, 26
PLANKTON 11, 20, 22-23
PLASTIC 10-11, 20-21, 24-26, 28-29
POLITICS 15-16
PROTESTS 7-9, 12, 15, 19, 21, 24-25

R
RAINBOW WARRIOR 9, 14, 24
ROSS SEA, THE 22-23, 25

S
SOCIAL MEDIA 18, 27
STOWE, DOROTHY 7
STOWE, IRVING 7

T
THOMPSON, EMMA 19
TOXIC CHEMICALS 8, 10, 12

V
VALUES 6
VOLUNTEERS 5, 9, 14-16, 18

W
WAR 4, 13

Photo Credits

GREENPEACE PHOTO CREDITS
Pg2 [©Greenpeace/Steve De Neef, Phillippines, 2013.] **Pg6** [©Greenpeace/Tim Aubry, USA, 2017.] **Pg7** [©Greenpeace/Bente Stachowske, Malta, 2017. ©Greenpeace/Robert Keziere, Canada, 1971. ©Greenpeace/Alan Katowitz, Canada, 2009.] **Pg8** [©Greenpeace/Hernan Vitenberg, Argentina, 2018.] **Pg9** [©Greenpeace/Tom Jefferson, Australia, 2013. ©Greenpeace/OneDrone, Slovenia, 2017.] **Pg12** [©Greenpeace/Ludolph Dahmen, Germany, 2015.] **Pg14** [©Greenpeace/Masaya Noda, Japan, 2015. ©Greenpeace/Denis Sinyakov, Russia, 2014. ©Greenpeace/Ben Deiman, Amsterdam, 2008. ©Greenpeace/Mark Meyer, Alaska, 2015.] **Pg18** [©Greenpeace/Ardiles Rante, Indonesia, 2009.] **Pg19** [©Greenpeace/John Cobb, London, 2015.] **Pg20** [©Greenpeace/Fred Dott, Germany, 2016.] **Pg21** [©Greenpeace/David Mirzoeff, UK, 2016. ©Greenpeace/Daniel Müller, Germany, 2016. ©Greenpeace/Daniel Müller, Germany, 2016.] **Pg23** [©Greenpeace/Chris Grodotzki, Germany, 2018.] **Pg24&25** [©Greenpeace/Bente Stachowske, Malta, 2017. ©Greenpeace/Pedro Armestre, Spain, 2017. ©Greenpeace/Will Rose, UK, 2019. ©Greenpeace/Köksal Mataraci, Istanbul, 2018. ©Greenpeace/Zoe Jeanne Burrell, Australia, 2018. ©Greenpeace, Philippines, 2017. ©Greenpeace/Clément Tardif, Senegal, 2012. ©Greenpeace/Francesco Alesi, Italy, 2010. ©Greenpeace/Samir Kayal, Beirut, 2017.]

Front Cover – Stu Shaw. 4 – Aysezgicmeli, Dmytro Zinkevych, Rawpixel.com. 5 – Rawpixel.com, Peeratouch Vatcharapanon, Alexander Raths. 6 – Kotomiti Okuma, yanatul. 8 – Scanrail1, Zhiltsov Alexandr, By Ethan Daniels, electra, Microgen. 10 – FloridaStock, Sasa Kadrijevic, Petr Klabal. 11 – kakteen, By Rich Carey. 12 & 13 – By Everett Historical, Vladimir Melnik, CHAIUDON. 16 – Casper1774 Studio. 19 – Jaguar PS. 20 – By FedBul, Oona M. Lönnstedt. 22 – By Rich Lindie, Mariusz Potocki, Dmytro Pylypenko, Christian Musat. 26&27 – keellla, glenda, Anatolii Riepin, Sylvie Bouchard, Syda Productions, Rawpixel.com. 28 – Roman Sinichkin, PhotoStock10, grey_and, Roman Stetsyk. Background on all pages: Flas100. Cardboard & Paper – Andrey_Kuzmin, Palokha Tetiana, NLshop, Picsfive, Andrey Eremin, Adam Cegledi, Flas100. ANATOL, Prostock-studio, Elena Polovinko.

Background on all pages: Flas100. Cardboard & Paper – Andrey_Kuzmin, Palokha Tetiana, NLshop, Picsfive, Andrey Eremin, Adam Cegledi, Flas100. ANATOL, Prostock-studio, Elena Polovinko.
Images are courtesy of Shutterstock.com. With thanks to Getty Images, Thinkstock Photo and iStockphoto.